May The Thoughts
Be With You

Ideas and wisdom to
inspire your days

By Charlotte Reed

HAY HOUSE

Carlsbad, California • New York City
London • Sydney • New Delhi

'Charlotte's book is like a warm ray of sunshine. Her wise tips for a better way to get through the day are insightful, inspiring and leave you with a smile on your face. It takes a sensitive soul to say things in just the right way to give you the paradigm shift you've been yearning for!'
NATALIE IMBRUGLIA, SINGER/SONGWRITER AND ACTRESS

'When I picked up a copy of *May The Thoughts Be With You*, the hairs on my arms stood on end: there was something immediately positive in the air, even though I had yet to open the book. When I did so, I couldn't stop turning the pages, absorbing a feeling of warmth, love and wellbeing as I did so, as I smiled and enjoyed each thought and its cheery accompanying image. By the end of the book, my first thought was all the people I could give copies to, all the people who would find their day a little bit easier and their smile a little wider thanks to this magical book.'
RACHEL KELLY, AUTHOR OF THE BESTSELLING MEMOIR *BLACK RAINBOW*

♥ This little book started its life as a self-published title which I used to sell at Portobello Road Market in Notting Hill, London. The book grew from there and a little while later global publisher Hay House offered me a wonderful publishing deal!

However, even though my book is now in lots of shops in various countries, I still sell it at my market stall, along with a range of related artwork too. This is because I genuinely love meeting my customers and Portobello Road is such a special place I wanted to remain part of its market community. If you'd like to visit the stall you can find details of when and where I trade on my website:

www.maythethoughtsbewithyou.com

love
Charlotte ♥

It is far more exciting
to create a miracle
than to wait for one
to happen.

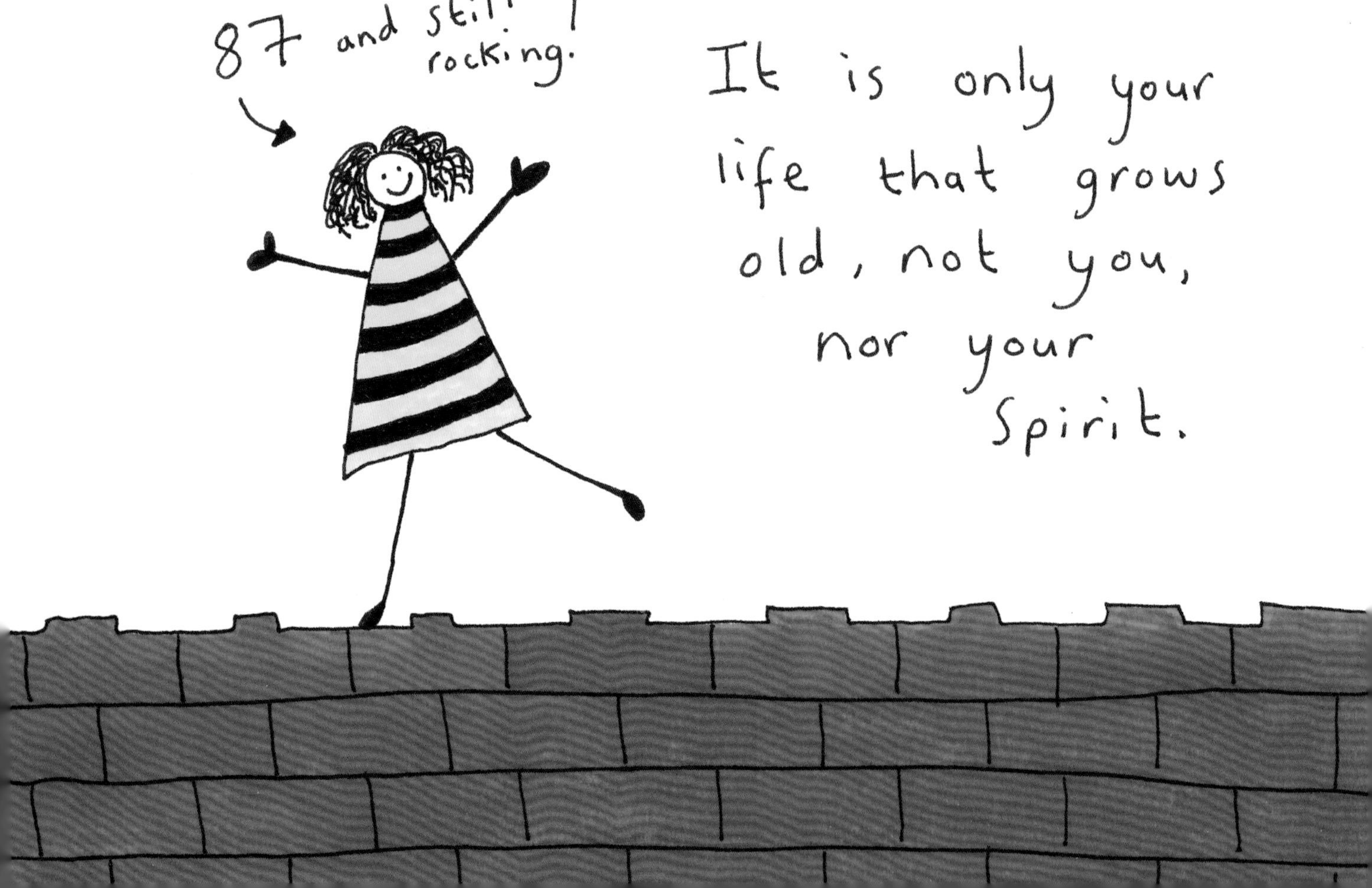

It is only your life that grows old, not you, nor your spirit.

When you die
you won't think of
how much money
you made, you will
think of how much
love you gave.

♥ If souls could speak, this is ♥ probably what they would say: 'Stop worrying! You CAN do it. Give yourself a break. You deserve it. TRUST. Why not? What are you waiting for? Stop caring what others think. DO IT! ENJOY IT! Oh yes, and one more small thing, I don't know how long I'm going to be in your body for, so for God's sake, MAKE THE MOST of it!!'

♥   ♥

never mind Stopping to look at the view, I've got to get to the top!
The end goal will feel meaningless if you've forgotten to enjoy the journey on the way.

The Professor of Truth

As far as I can see it, there are no disadvantages of being friendly, approachable and kind. A polite, genuine attitude will not only serve others well but it will serve you well too!

Daily ritual for stress - free living:
Do your best then let the universe do the rest!

you have a choice: Conform to someone else's way, or you CAN FORM your own way.

The wise are those who have travelled to the depths of their tragedies and then returned from them, bearing a gift for the world in their hands.

Clever Cat

Happiness is not something lucky people are blessed by, it's a state of mind – you choose it, it doesn't choose you.

It is when our plans go 'wrong' that wonderful, unforeseen things are allowed to occur.

When you've learnt something worthwhile, remember to always be an ambassador of it.

Simple Yet True

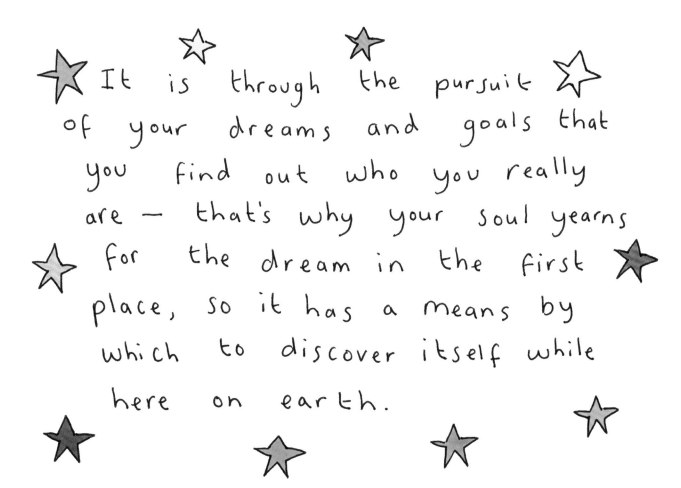

It is through the pursuit of your dreams and goals that you find out who you really are — that's why your soul yearns for the dream in the first place, so it has a means by which to discover itself while here on earth.

You can still be compassionate, calm, kind and understanding even in the most terrible of situations, in fact, this is when you need to be these things the most.

Nobody said modern-day life had to be busy or stressful. The pace you go is up to you.

wise
Our lives are not full of problems, they are full of learning opportunities.

Contrary to popular belief, being hard on yourself will not make you strong, but being kind to yourself WILL.

If you dig deep enough, you will always find love at the source of everything.
I knew it was under there somewhere!
LOVE

So often we want to make something bigger, better, more special or more successful and forget we can enjoy it exactly as it is.

Often the biggest and best changes in life are only the smallest of steps away.

no matter how rich and successful you become, it's still a good idea to take the bus and unblock your own drains.

money bags →

Be brave and follow what <u>you</u> believe instead.

Letting go of control is necessary if one is to experience the true meaning of FREEDOM!

Honouring someone's freedom is one of the greatest gifts you can give them.

Call yourself bad names for long enough and your mind will start to believe them (luckily this also works for good names too!).

Don't worry if you lose your power, you may find you're stronger without it.

when you get attached to the result you miss out on all the magic...

The Wise Worm

What does
P.E.A.C.E mean?
Maybe it means
the Power to
Emancipate And
Change Everyone.

The blocks that keep you from being your potential are not in the outer world, they are inside you. They stem from wrong thoughts you have like: 'I'm not good enough,' 'I'm not creative enough' and 'I could never do that AND make it work.' The list goes on! The trick is to challenge these thoughts so they disappear - then you can watch the outer world magically shift in accordance with these inner changes.

An equation we weren't taught in School

Self-Sabotage and self-judgement are very cleverly disguised strains of the procrastination virus.

There is a reason why history
Keeps repeating itself; there
is something more or something
else to learn.

Pay attention to your dreams at night, they have a lot to tell you about what's going on in your life and the symbolism of them can actually be a preview of your future.

If you believe in magic more, then more magic will come true for you.

Money only makes people happy if they've earned it doing what they love.

You will never live your heart's desires or create an authentic life as long as you comply with living someone else's reality.

Our most fundamental journey in life is not the journey of success and wealth, it is the journey of exploring the self.

Your intuition is like a muscle, the more you use it the stronger it gets.

A change of perspective is as good as a rest.

How can you expect to get what you want if you're not prepared to turn down what you don't want?..

pain generally won't go away if
we ignore it, but will if we
get to know it.

The Happy Hippy

Life only changes because your soul is ready for a change.

SIMPLE YET TRUE

Accepting change
and taking risks
are the key ingredients
to leading a full
life.

The Professor of Truth

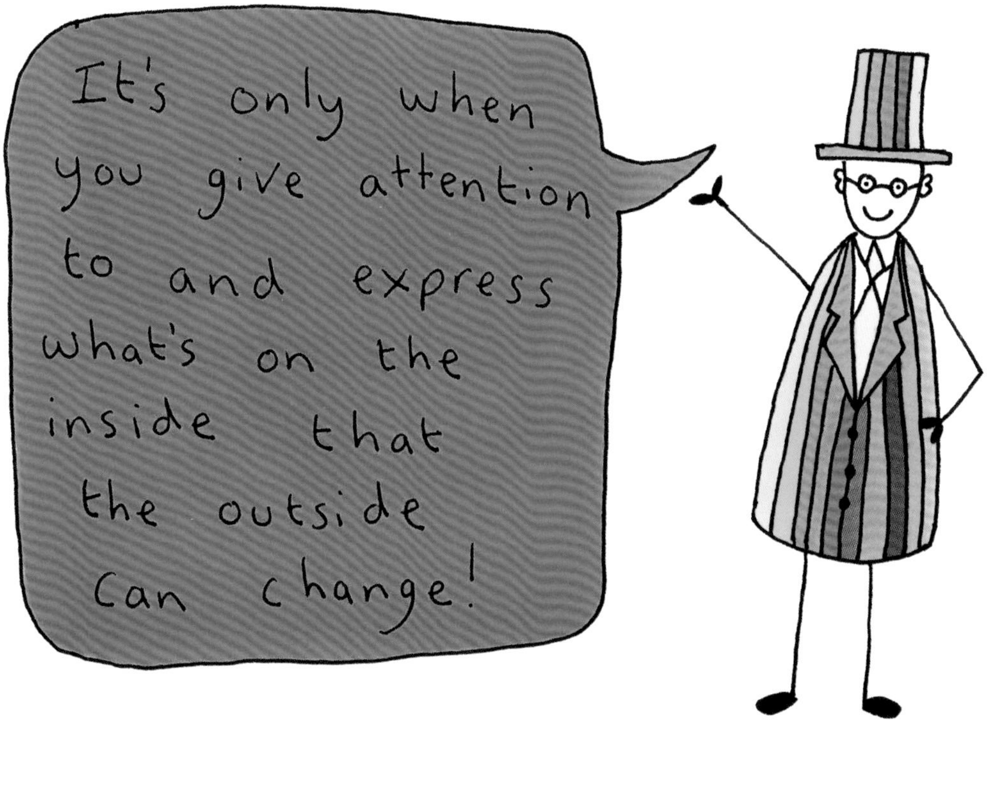

Burt, you're always so happy and cheerful - what's your secret??
Well, every morning, the first thing I do is have a cup of this special brew. It's called positivitea!

10 ideas for a life of no regrets:

1. Live a life true to <u>you</u>, no one else.
2. Laugh heartily whenever you can.
3. Cherish your friendships (they're your support network).
4. Invite silliness in.
5. Create! (It's what keeps your soul happy.)
6. Work hard, but not too hard.
7. Spend time with the ones you love.
8. Be COURAGEOUS, inspire people with your talents.
9. Practise being kind and generous towards others (even strangers).
10. Have the eyes of a child, even when you're old.

Do not be scared to look within. Although the waters of your soul may appear murky and uninviting, there could be real treasure at the bottom waiting to be discovered.

Chest of potential

When doing something creative, it's quite normal to feel judgemental, vulnerable and shameful of it afterwards. The ones who go on to make creative careers and lives are the ones who give their vulnerability some love and then carry on regardless.

Remember, you can always ask the universe for help.

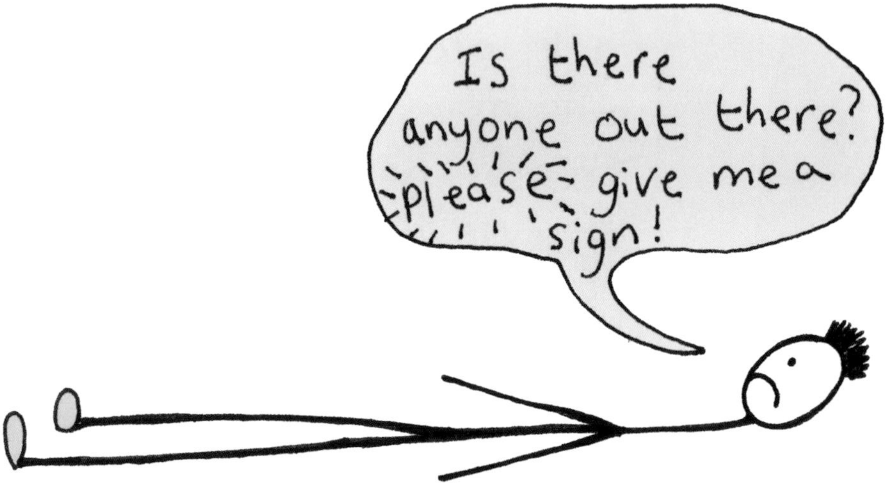

The Shoeless Guru

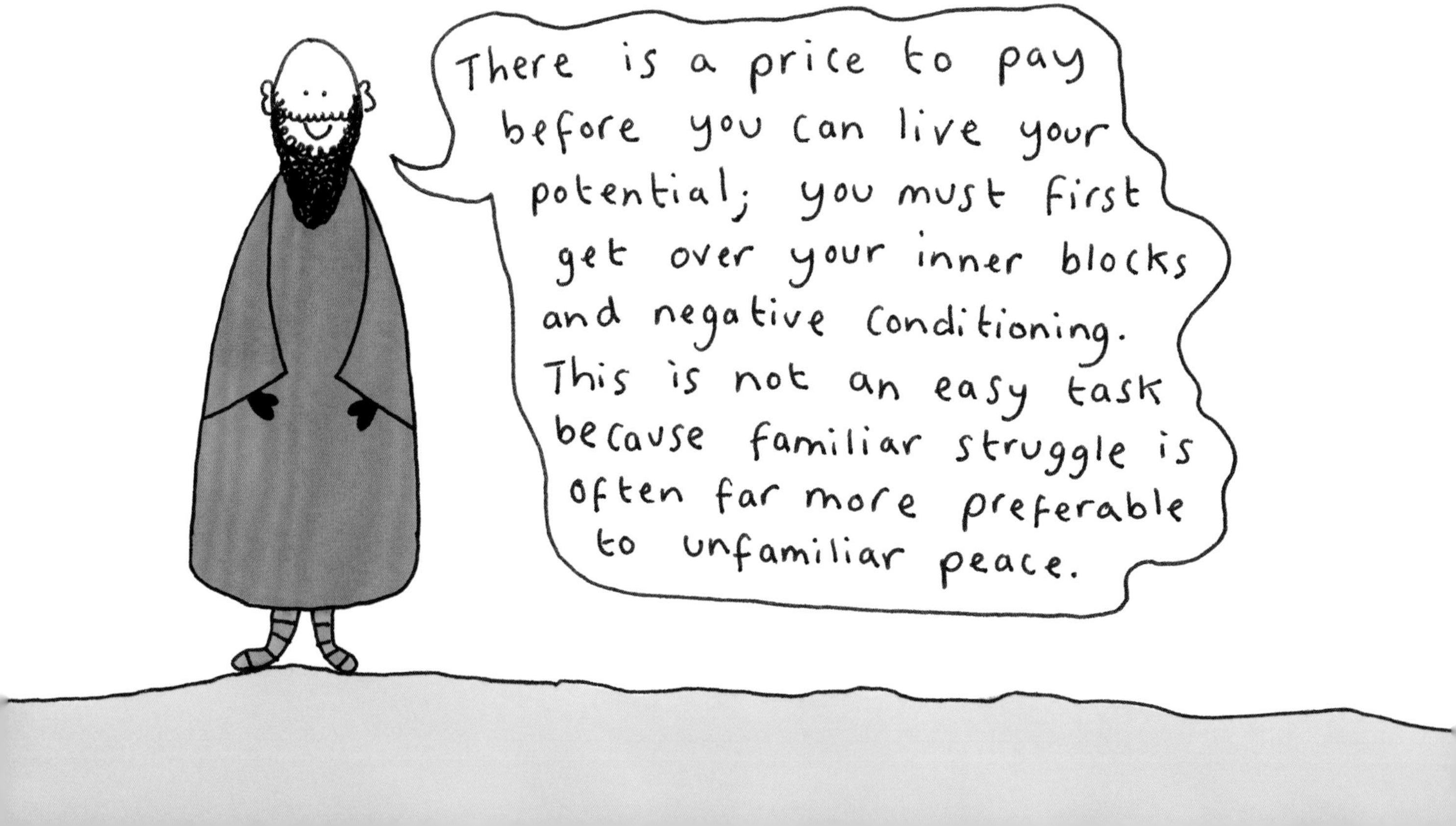

Thoughts are very powerful things. Think them often enough and long enough and they'll become self-fulfilling prophecies.

If you're having trouble living in the moment and being fully present, try hanging out with some wise gurus and 'present moment' practitioners, otherwise known as children.

Souls are like dogs, they love to be taken on walks in nature.

The more you grow as a person the more humble you'll find yourself becoming— someone who is forever in awe of the magical mystery that is life.

2014
Wish list
1. Richer
2. Thinner
3. Find lover

2015
Wish list
1. Richer
2. Thinner

2016
Wish list
1. Richer
2. Thinner

2017
Wish list
1. Richer
2. Thinner
3. leave lover

2018
Wish list
1. Richer
2. Thinner
3. Find new lover

2019
~~Wish~~ list
1. START LIVING!

Deep down, you know what to do, you know what to say, you know how to be and you know all the answers to your problems... Why else do you think you've got a soul?

One of the most liberating things you can do is not get attached to results.

The most truthful of words are not heard with the ear, they are felt with the heart.

The Professor of Truth

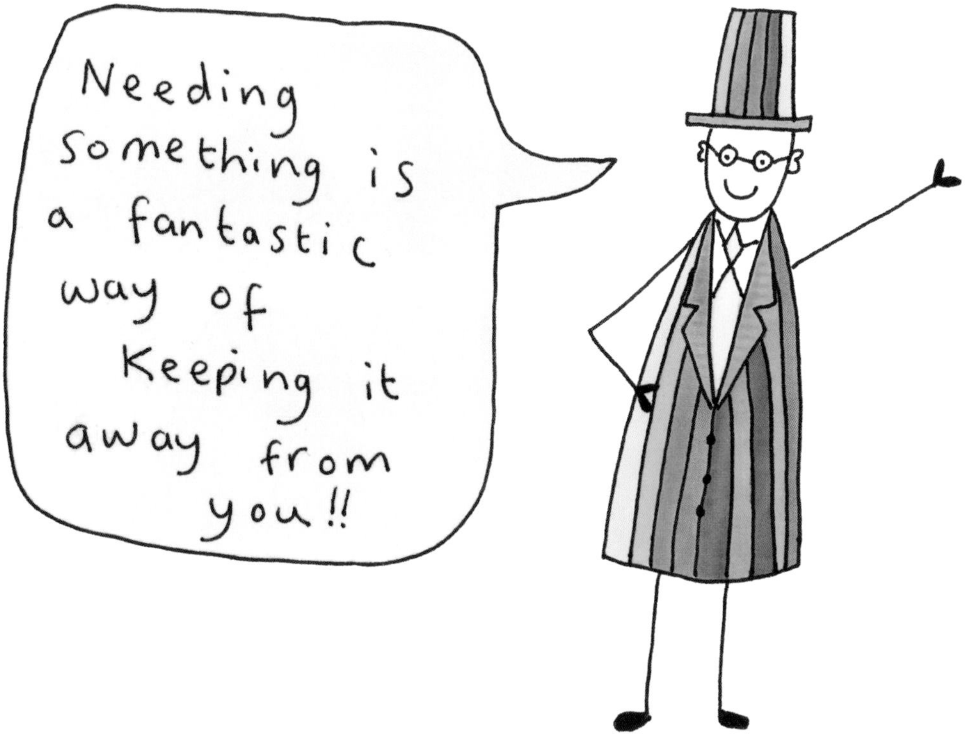

Although often difficult at first, change usually turns us into a beautiful thing.

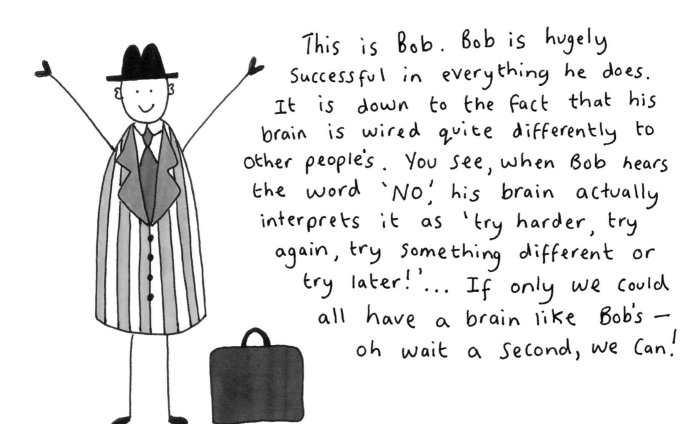

This is Bob. Bob is hugely successful in everything he does. It is down to the fact that his brain is wired quite differently to other people's. You see, when Bob hears the word 'NO', his brain actually interprets it as 'try harder, try again, try something different or try later!'... If only we could all have a brain like Bob's — oh wait a second, we can!

labels are very dangerous and should come with warning labels!

The Wise Worm

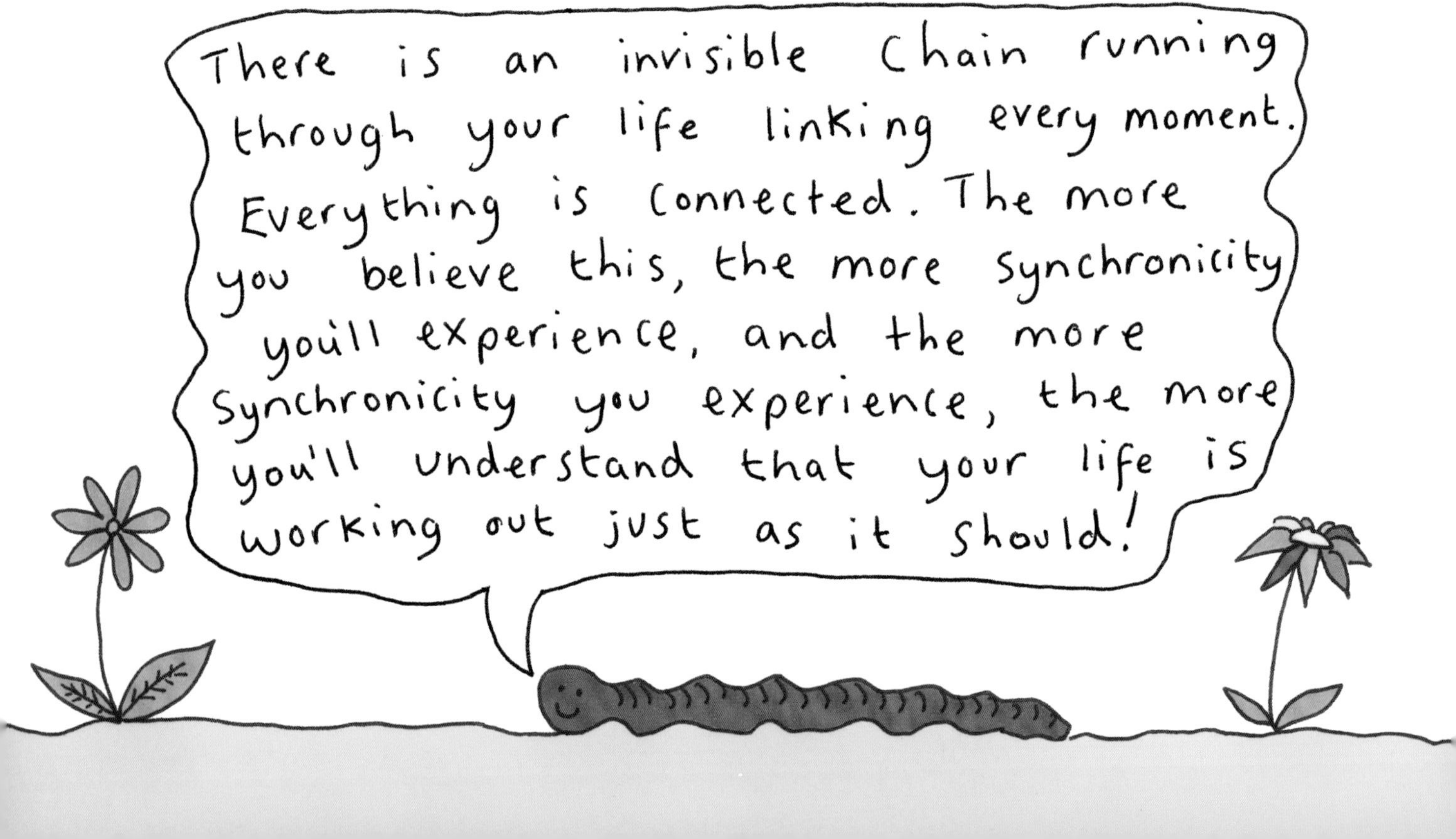

Imperfection
is the
truest
form
of beauty.

often in life, your Plan B turns out to be the best thing for you. Maybe the `B´ stands for 'blessing'.

♥ Your job is not who you are. ♥ Your clothes are not who you are. Your money (or lack of) is not who you are. Your home is not who you are, and neither is your car. It is your heart, your soul, your spirit and your very essence that make ♥ YOU WHO YOU ARE. ♥

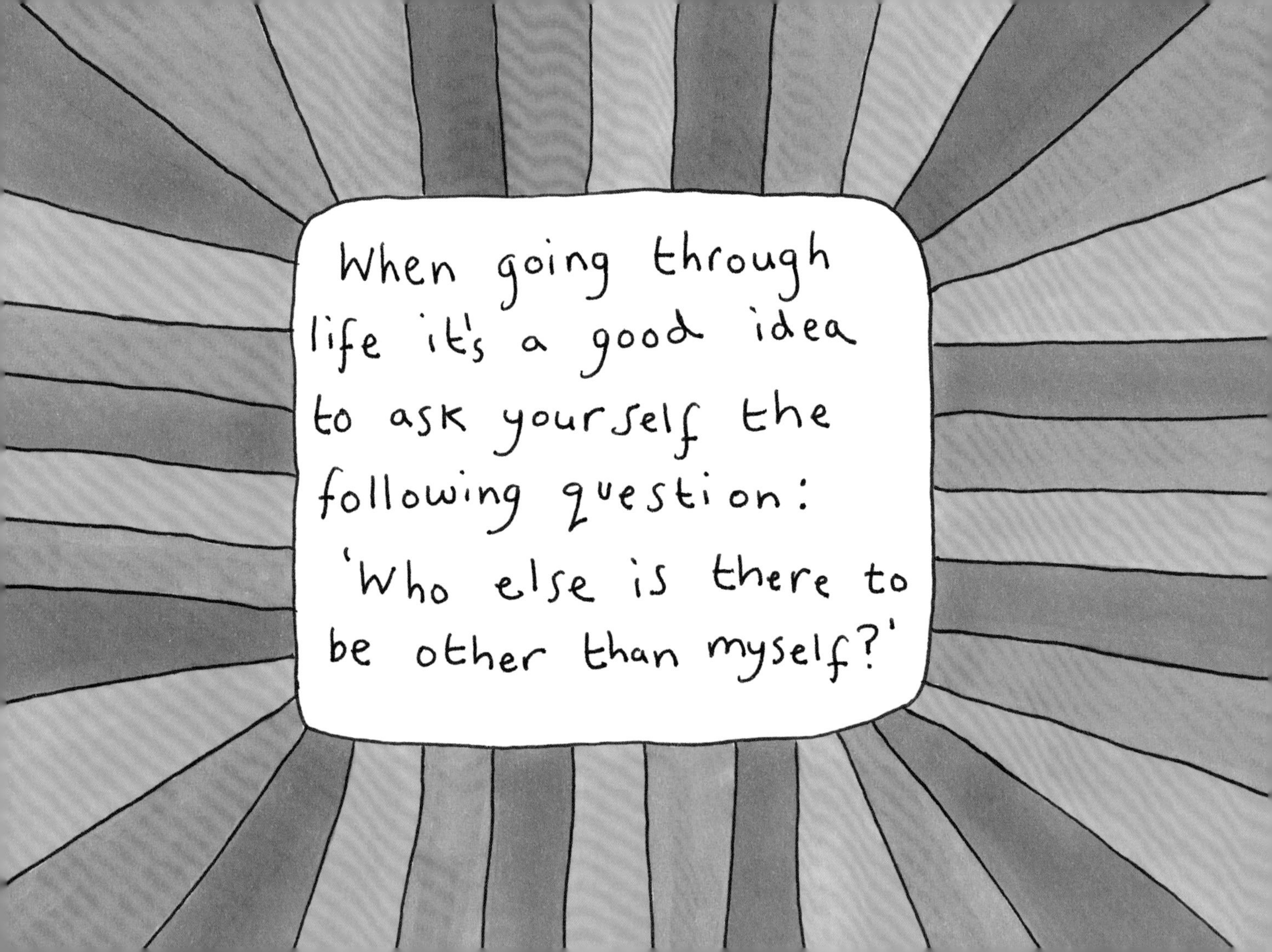

When going through
life it's a good idea
to ask yourself the
following question:
'Who else is there to
be other than myself?'

falling in love with someone is wonderful, but falling in love with yourself is where the magic begins.

you
can
be as
free as
me.

What things would you do if you didn't feel you had to judge your result? Would you finally start painting, singing, writing, dancing, acting, photography? Start enjoying your creativity, instead of expecting to create a masterpiece.

The Shoeless Guru

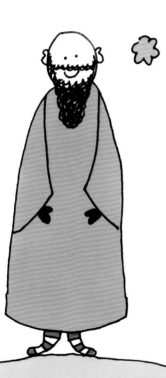

The more I know the less I need to know.

Wisdom means not needing to understand...

At the end of their lives, people often wish that they'd let themselves be happier.

The limits we have given ourselves will be part of us until the day we realise they are not.

Do not get attached to all that is 'good' in your life, and deny all that is 'bad.' The key is to love it all in all its glory — then you are truly alive.

Sadly, some people spend their whole lives thinking 'what if this happens?', 'what if that happens?', 'what if this goes wrong?', 'what if that goes wrong?', and then die having never really lived.

Your home
always was,
always is
and always
will be,
inside you...

yeah!

Life is too short and too precious to waste it all on being stuck in our issues.
wise

It is only you who knows how to love yourself completely.

There is still magic in the mundane.

Food ☑

Water ☑

Shelter ☑

family ☑

friends ☑

bus fare ☑

Luckily for all of us, very little is needed to make a happy life.

If you enjoyed this book then further thoughts can be found on social media.

Links to my pages can be found on my website :

 www.maythethoughtsbewithyou.com

If you want to purchase more books or this book's related artwork then please also visit my website.

Photographer: Nathan Browning

Hello, I'm Charlotte, the creator of May The Thoughts Be With You. I thought I'd share the story of how this book came about, just in case you were interested!

Although this book is full of positivity, it actually originated from a period of depression I had back in 2008. Let me explain! The depression was the most horrific, difficult and frightening time of my life. Anyone who's suffered with this terrible condition will know how utterly helpless it makes you feel. I was offered medication to get well but even at my worst points, I knew that wasn't the right path for me. I've nothing against anti-depressants but my instincts were telling me to get better the natural way, and I did that by talking to understanding people, eating very healthily, walking for 1-2 hours every day and having regular acupuncture. There was something else that helped me recover too, something that actually turned into my passion and slowly revealed itself as my life's work. About two months into the depression. I started to write my own happy and positive thoughts each day. I wrote them to remind myself what I was supposed to feel like, and that while I couldn't see it, life was still a wonderful thing. I then shared my thought each morning as my Facebook status, in case anything I was writing could benefit friends too. Over the two years of posting, I gathered quite a following. By then I'd fully recovered from the depression but I'd enjoyed writing my thoughts so much that I'd simply continued to do them. Friends had also started to ask if I could turn my thoughts into a book, and while it was a lovely idea, it didn't occur to me to actually do it!

Then suddenly, life tried to communicate with me. I was working in an office at the time and I developed Chronic Repetitive Strain Injury. The very painful condition meant I couldn't work for two years and eventually it became clear I'd never be able to return to my role. I needed a total life change. And then it dawned on me, maybe I should take my friends' advice and create a book of my thoughts? I got excited, the R.S.I. meant I could no longer use a computer but I knew handwriting the text would be fine... and maybe I could illustrate the thoughts too? I only had a basic drawing ability but that could make the book entertaining as well as meaningful! It seemed like a great idea. And that was it, my new life had begun; I resigned from my job, created the book, self-published it and then started selling it to anyone who was kind enough to buy a copy.

Initially, I sold 200 books to family, friends and friends of friends. Their feedback was incredibly encouraging so I decided to approach some local, independent book and gift shops, to see if they'd take some books. I was so nervous to ask them but to my delight they all said yes, and they even put the book by the till so everyone could see it. The book then became popular very quickly and in some shops it was their bestseller!

By that time, my friend had kindly built me a

Website and I was selling lots of copies through my online shop as well. I then had the idea of taking a stall at Portobello market in London's Notting Hill. I also picked my favourite thoughts from the book and enlarged them to sell as mounted prints. I was astounded. Customers would smile with delight as they leafed through the book's pages, giggling away at the drawings, and some even burst into tears because they said the thoughts spoke to them so much! And then there were the people who'd buy a book or a print and come back a few hours later to buy more. They said they knew someone who'd like my cheery work; a family member with a chronic illness, a friend in hospital, a sister with a broken heart, a depressed boyfriend, a lonely neighbour, a daughter who wanted a career change, a brother with P.T.S.D., a best friend going through rehab, a son with autism or simply a friend whose birthday was approaching. I was totally shocked. My little book, which had originated from such a dark, sad and lonely time in my life was being enjoyed and appreciated by lots of people. It was such a lovely feeling. And of course, because Portobello Road is such a tourist destination it really helped spread the word about my book. People from all around the world suddenly started ordering from my online shop, saying they'd bought a book at my stall and wanted more for family and friends.

Every part of my book's journey was a surprise but what surprised me the most was how popular the book was with children. Of course I'd written it with adults in mind but customers would tell me how much their children had enjoyed it too, and countless teachers were buying it to teach their pupils how to think more positively.

After a year and a half since launching my book, the word had spread so much I'd sold 5,000 copies, and even celebrities and royalty had come to my stall to purchase one! By that point a successful business woman called Shaa Wasmund had told global publisher Hay House about me. When the publisher contacted me to offer me a publishing deal I was ecstatic! Now my book is available in multiple countries and has even been translated into different languages. However, even though my book is now widely available I still continue to sell it at my market stall... I'd enjoyed doing it so I thought why not carry on?!

So that's the story so far. What wonderful things can spring from difficult times. Of course, I now look back at my depression and R.S.I. with different eyes. I see them as gifts. Yes, they were horrible, painful conditions to go through but they changed my life for the better because they helped me discover my true self and true happiness.

I very much hope that by reading my story you'll feel better or inspired in some way, or if you're going through a tough time, I hope you feel there may be a positive reason for it in the end and that your pain can become your strength. I'll say goodbye for now but as I'm still running my stall maybe I'll see you there one day! I certainly hope so. May the thoughts be with you, lots of love Charlotte 🖤

♥ Dedication ♥

I dedicate this book to all the people who believed in it when it was just an idea and then all the people who bought it when it was self-published: My family, friends, stall customers, online customers and the independent book and gift shops - you gave the book such a fantastic start! A huge thank you to Shaa and everyone at Hay House for giving me the life-changing opportunity of having it traditionally published.

I'd like to say thank you from the bottom of my heart to my sister Kate, who quite honestly walked every single step of the depression with me. A gigantic thank you also to my wonderful mum, dad, brother Rich, my dear friend Johnny Lucas and the rest of my family; Granso, Uncle I, Johnny May, Jacob, Zeb and Jahryn - I love you all so much!

Cheerio!

First published and distributed in the United Kingdom by:
Hay House UK Ltd, Astley House, 33 Notting Hill Gate, London W11 3JQ
Tel: +44 (0)20 3675 2450; Fax: +44 (0)20 3675 2451
www.hayhouse.co.uk

Published and distributed in the United States of America by:
Hay House Inc., PO Box 5100, Carlsbad, CA 92018-5100
Tel: (1) 760 431 7695 or (800) 654 5126
Fax: (1) 760 431 6948 or (800) 650 5115
www.hayhouse.com

Published and distributed in Australia by:
Hay House Australia Ltd, 18/36 Ralph St, Alexandria NSW 2015
Tel: (61) 2 9669 4299; Fax: (61) 2 9669 4144
www.hayhouse.com.au

Published and distributed in India by:
Hay House Publishers India, Muskaan Complex, Plot No.3, B-2,
Vasant Kunj, New Delhi 110 070
Tel: (91) 11 4176 1620; Fax: (91) 11 4176 1630
www.hayhouse.co.in

May the Thoughts Be with You® is a registered trademark.

A catalogue record for this book is available from the British Library.

ISBN: 978-1-78817-301-8

Printed in Italy